Draw Manga Extreme

Author: Heather Dakota

Illustrator: Ron Lim

Designer: Bill Henderson

an imprint of
SCHOLASTIC
www.scholastic.com

Scholastic and Tangerine Press and associated logos are trademarks of Scholastic Inc

Published by Tangerine Press, an imprint of
Scholastic Inc; 557 Broadway; New York, NY 10012

10 9 8 7 6 5 4 3 2

ISBN 0-439-78281-3

Printed and bound in China

How to Develop Characters

Before you get started drawing characters you need to "develop" them. Character development is a fancy way to say how your character dresses, his or her personality, and maybe where he or she is from.

The inspirations for your characters can come from just about anywhere. Look at your family and friends — would they make good manga characters?

As the ideas start coming to you, start to imagine how to dress your character and what he or she looks like. Bet your mind is working on it now, so grab a pencil and let's get started.

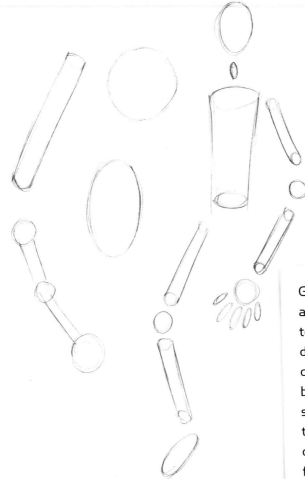

Get out your pencils and scribble a little bit to see what they can do. All of the manga characters in this book start off with simple shapes: sticks, tubes, ovals, and circles. Try drawing a few of these shapes.

Materials

All the materials you need to get started are included in your kit!

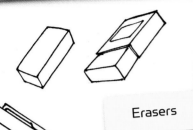

Erasers

The eraser that comes with your kit is a good one, but you'll have to erase easy or you might tear your paper. Soft, kneaded erasers used by professional artists are available at art supply stores.

Fine Tip Marker

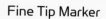

The fine tip marker in your kit is perfect for inking your drawings. When you have completed your drawings, inking it will make it look professional. When the ink has dried (only a few minutes), erase all your pencil lines and you'll have a great-looking finished drawing!

Pencils

Pencils come in different hardnesses. With your kit, you get HB, 3H, 5H, and 6H pencils. The softer pencils make dark lines and are hard to erase. The HB pencil is the softest in your kit.

Mini Markers and Ruler

The mini markers in your kit are for coloring your characters. Just don't leave the marker in one spot too long or the ink will bleed through the paper! You can find a bigger variety of color markers at art supply stores.

The ruler is to help you draw guidelines and backgrounds.

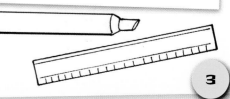

Drawing a Boy Character

Let's start out with a basic body layout using simple shapes. Make big circles for the hands, feet, and midsection, a large circle for the head, and small circles for the joints at the shoulder, elbows, and knees. Connect these circles with lines that will eventually make the arms, legs, body, and neck.

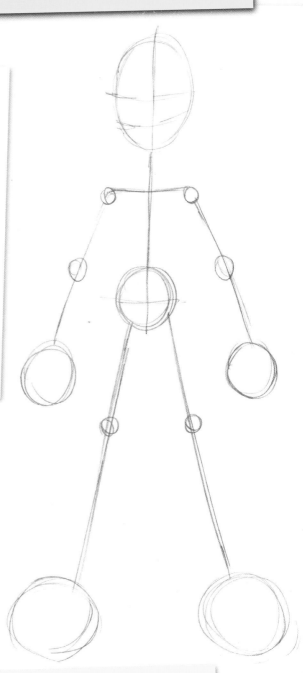

This is how to lay out the pose of your character.

Add Body Definition

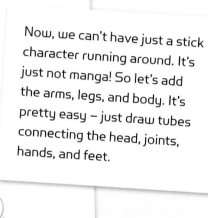

Now, we can't have just a stick character running around. It's just not manga! So let's add the arms, legs, and body. It's pretty easy – just draw tubes connecting the head, joints, hands, and feet.

Are you finding it difficult to draw exactly what you're seeing in the book? There are no rules that say you can't copy the drawing. So, go ahead and trace it! The more you trace, the more your hands and brain will get used to seeing and drawing. Tracing is just another way to practice.

Character style

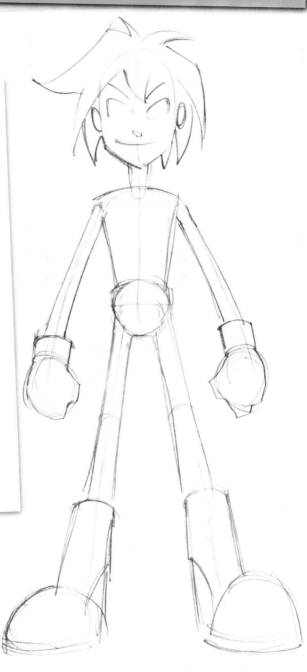

Let's give this character some style! It's going to be a good hair day, so give this guy some hot spikes. You don't need to get too detailed on the facial features yet, so just roughly sketch them in. Don't forget your character's clothing style. Keep in mind what your character does, his personality, and any special powers he might have.

Finished Character

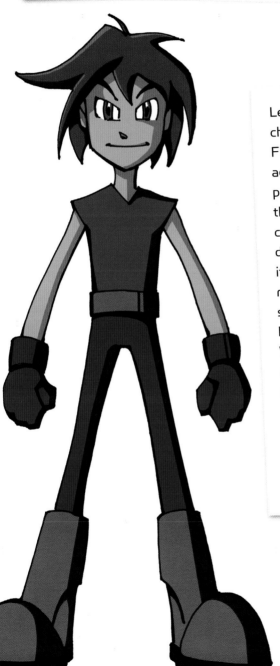

Let's finish off those character details. Finalize the eyes by adding the iris and pupils. Add detail to the clothing, and, cool, the drawing is done! Now, you want it to look professional, right? So, go over your sketch lines with a black fine-tip marker. When the ink is dry, erase your sketch lines, and add color.

Man, you have made a cool character! Great job! But I think he needs a companion...

Drawing a Girl Character

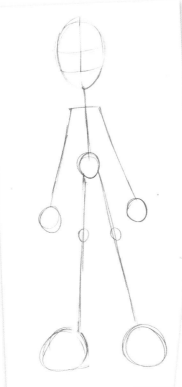

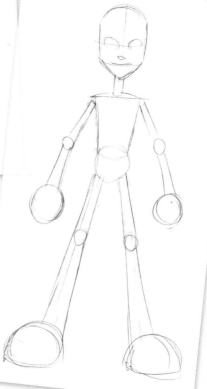

Manga girls are a little different to draw than boys – the biggest difference being that girls are tapered differently.

Add Body Definition

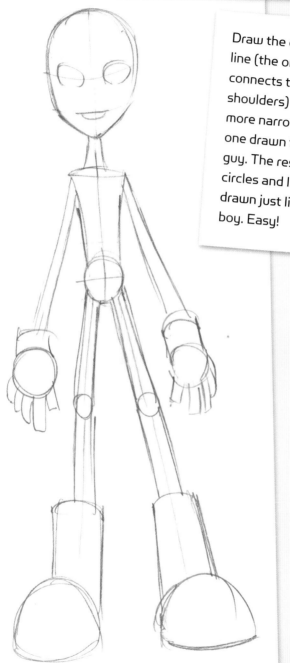

Draw the collarbone line (the one that connects the shoulders) a little more narrow than the one drawn for the guy. The rest of the circles and lines are drawn just like the boy. Easy!

Character Style

Girl style is different than boy style. Duh! Here's where you'll make changes. The hair is longer. The lines that form the torso are thinner, giving the girl a slight curve, and the arms and legs are thinner and taper more than on the boy drawing.

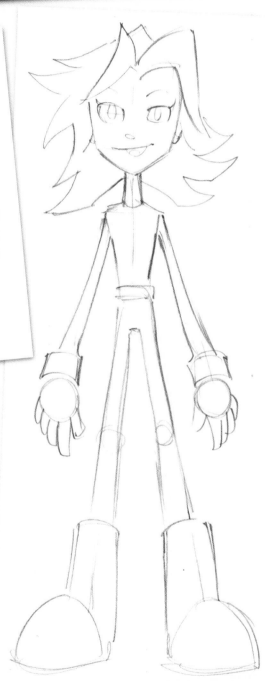

Finished Character

Now, make the character look like a girl by adding more eyelashes, a small nose, and maybe some accessories. Ink, erase, color, and you've got it!

Manga Action!

Running

Jumping

Here are some characters in different poses. Manga characters don't just stand stiffly in the corner, so get them into action! And don't forget if you are having trouble drawing these action poses, you can just try tracing them instead.

Create as many poses as you can. Keep practicing and have fun!

Dancing

Male Head Front View

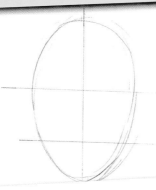

Start out with an egg-shaped oval, draw vertical guidelines through the center of the oval, then draw 2 horizontal guidelines, one about halfway down and the other about ¾ of the way down the face. These lines will help you place the eyes and mouth.

Sketch basic features like the eyes, nose, and mouth. Use the guidelines to keep the eyes and mouth even. Add the nose in the middle. And make the chin a little pointier.

Define the features a little more and sketch the hair. You can add an expression like a smile or frown. And don't forget the ears. He has to hear!

Finish the details by drawing the pupils and putting in eyebrows. Add details to the ears. Erase your sketch lines and you are finished!

Male Head Side View

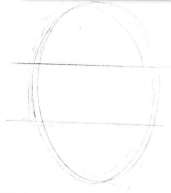

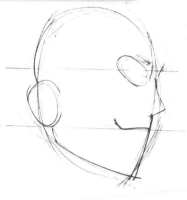

The shape of the head is slightly different for this view. Notice the chin juts out from the head, so it should look like an unbalanced shape.

Make a mini triangle coming off the face for the nose. Sketch in the eye and one ear.

The eyes are angled differently than in the front view. See page 21 for more details. Sketch a slight protrusion to indicate the forehead.

Continue to define the features and hair, until you like how it looks!

Female Head Front View

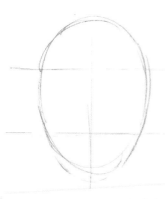

Draw the same kind of shape as you did for the male head front view.

Note that the female forehead is rounder than the angular forehead of the male.

Add eyes with lashes and hair. Draw a small, smooth nose for the female.

And don't forget the more classic eyes of a female character. See page 21 for more detail.

These are samples of different kinds of heads you can draw for your characters. And don't worry if you're having trouble; just copy a few of these down!

Expressions

Characters have feelings, too, of course! Here are a few expressions for male faces. See how much changing the eyebrows and mouth changes the expression?

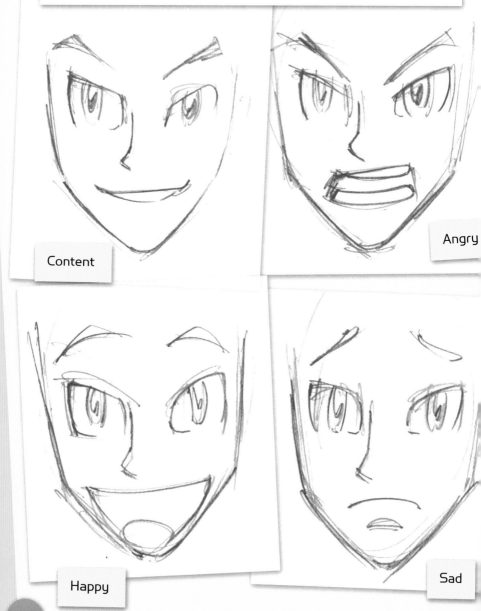

Content

Angry

Happy

Sad

Now practice these expressions with a female's face.

Content

Angry

Happy

Sad

The Face Says It All!

Here are some more expressions you can try. Play with different expressions with the different head views. You're sure to come up with lots of different expressions! Don't get frustrated- faces are hard to draw. If you are still having trouble drawing freehand keep practicing and tracing the drawings in the book.

The Eyes

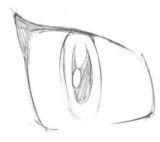

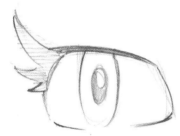

There are a few different styles of eyes for manga drawings. Take a look at the examples here. You can vary your eyes with different eyelashes, pupils, and eyebrows.

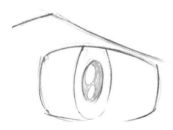

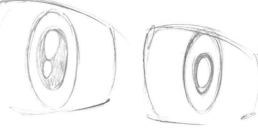

Check out the close-up
of this character's pupil!
When you breakdown
the shapes, it's not so
hard.

And when you're drawing
from the side, here's what
the eyes look like.

It's a Good Hair Day

Here are some hairstyles for the guys! Check out how spiky the tips are. Manga characters typically have really cool hair.

Girl characters have similarly spiky hair. Remember, no hair is too wild for manga characters!

How to Draw Legs

Start out with the basic line drawing for the leg and then add the circles for the hip and knee joints. Next, add the tubing to the legs and feet to give them some dimension.

Here's a side view.

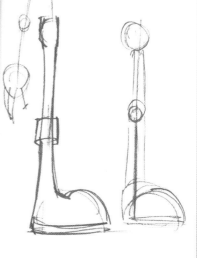

Here is an example of a front view of the legs.

If you add nuts and bolts, you can draw a robot leg like this one!

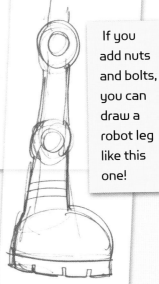

Leg Poses

Here are a few different poses for the legs. You can put them in any position just by changing where you put the joint circles and leg tubes.

Running

Sitting

Kicking

These Feet Were Made for Walkin'!

Here's how you draw some feet for your characters. Start by sketching basic shapes. Once you have the basic shapes done, add the little details in the shoes (or bare feet).

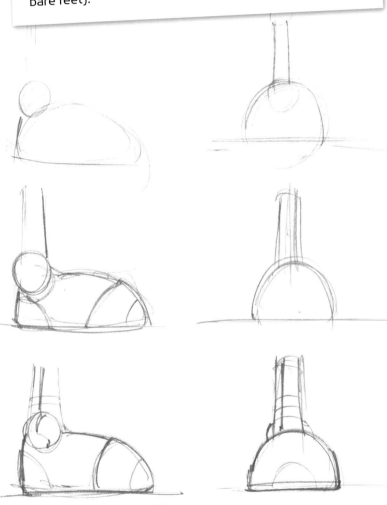

Foot with shoe side view

Foot with shoe front view

There are all kinds of feet you can add to your manga character. Don't forget to keep in mind your character's style, personality, and surroundings. Some characters might have shoes, some might be barefoot, and some might even have only two toes!

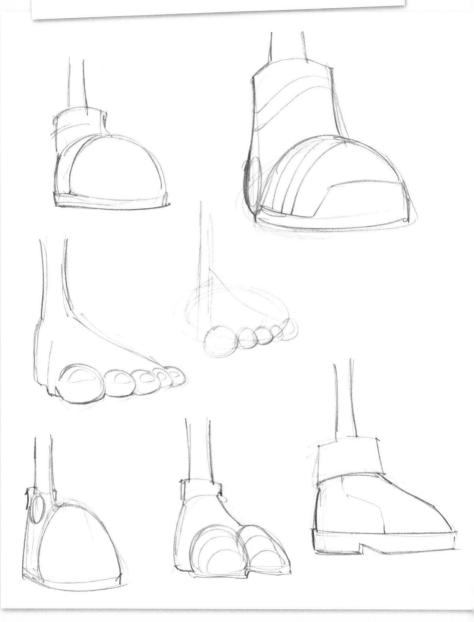

Can You Give Me a Hand?

Hands are not the easiest body parts to draw, but when you break it down into simple shapes, it gets a whole lot easier.

Start out with a circle and five lines for the fingers. That's pretty easy right?

Finish the fingers by creating tubes and connect them to the circle.

Erase where the fingers connect to the circle and your hand is almost done.

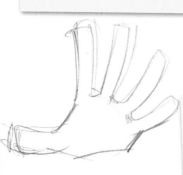

Just flatten out the bottom of the circle to form the palm and you have your finished hand! See, that wasn't too hard, right?

Top View of Hand

Palm up or down, it's still done the same way! Start with the sticks and circles. Then make the sticks into tubes. Connect the tubes and add the details. Not too shabby there! You're getting good!

More Hands!

Hands can be put in all kinds of different positions. If you have trouble drawing these hands, don't worry, it just takes practice, practice, practice.

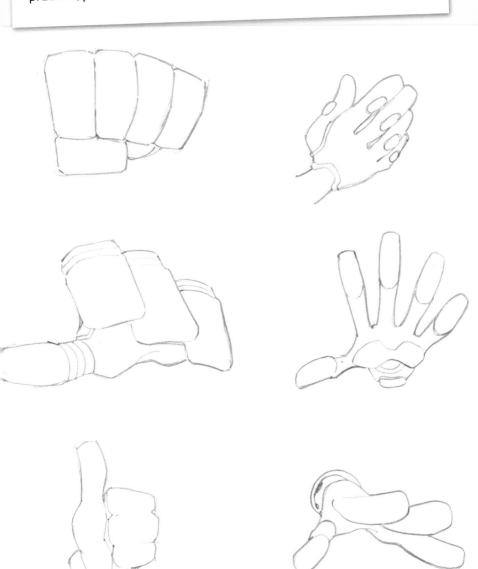

Arms

Arms are pretty easy to draw. All you have to do is connect the shoulder to the elbow, and the elbow to the hand.
Make skinny or muscular arms by changing the thickness.
No problem, right?

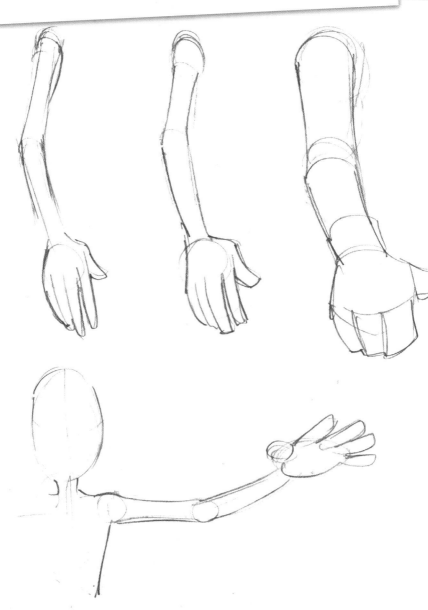

More Manga Characters!

Here are six special characters for you to draw. Use the techniques you just learned, but most of all have fun! If you get frustrated, just take a deep breath and try tracing the characters. No worries!

Kid Hero

This action hero is confident, brave, and ready to take on any villain – just like you (except for maybe the villain part)! This character is made up of sharp angles (just look at the hair!). The body shape is the basic boy style shown on page 4, and his face shows a happy-go-lucky personality.

Start with your basic shapes and then add the tubes!

Wow! You're good! Look what you drew! Kid Hero is ready for action!

Cat Girl

Look at all the circles and sticks. See how they're placed? This is going to be a manga character in action!

Cat Girl is a character type that is super fun to draw. Her female form is a lot like the girl that was drawn on page 8. This character has a lot of cat energy so keep that in mind as you draw her. You will also need to draw the ears and tail of a cat, and the oversized gloves. She has a very mischievous personality (check out her eyes!).

Boy you're getting good! Don't forget to ink your drawing and erase the sketch lines for a professional look.

What? You're still having problems with drawing freehand? Don't worry about it! Drawing takes a lot practice. Just trace it see how the parts together.

Captain Space

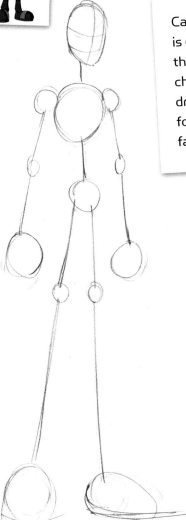

Captain Space is a strong leader. He is older, wiser, and much taller than the other characters. He is a futuristic character, so keep that in mind as you're drawing his clothes. This character's form should be long and lean with strong facial features.

Oh look, more sticks and circles! You know what to do. Make your tubes and add some details!

Very cool! He
looks ready
for action. Ink
the drawing
and erase the
sketch marks.
Great job!
Now just add
a little color.

Hunter

Hunter hails from an acient tribe of warriors. His face and arms are marked with tribal symbols. He is even more angular than Kid Hero and has lots of sharp edges. He is a fearless and strong fighter, so don't forget his battle staff!

Fabulous job! Keep up the good work! Don't forget to ink the drawing, erase the sketch lines, and add some color!

Archer

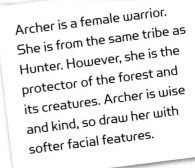

Archer is a female warrior. She is from the same tribe as Hunter. However, she is the protector of the forest and its creatures. Archer is wise and kind, so draw her with softer facial features.

Awesome Job!
Keep it up and keep
practicing!

Gray Thunder

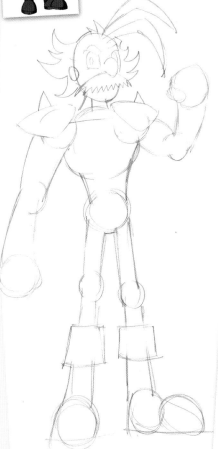

Gray Thunder will help you learn how to draw an older character. He is both warrior and teacher. You'll have fun drawing his unique face, mustache, and big, round nose.

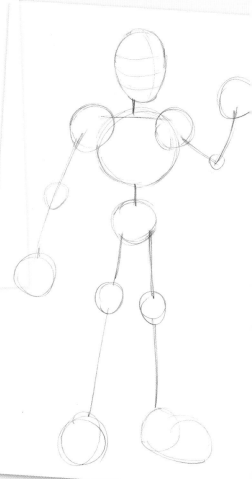

It looks like it's getting easier for you! Your practicing is paying off!

Foreshortening
a matter of perspective

Foreshortening is a fancy way to say "coming out at you." Look at all the drawings on this page. See how the fingers and feet look like they are coming out at you – that's because of the perspective. Here's how you do it:

Draw the tubes that you would for the arms and legs, but overlap them a little bit. Make the part that is overlapping a little bigger than the part underneath. Then draw the part that is closest to you, like the hands and feet, the largest. This gives the impression that the part on top is very close to you. Here are some samples for you to try. Foreshortening is not an easy thing to do, so try tracing these a few times first.

Use foreshortening to emphasize an action in your drawings. Look at the foreshortening used in these characters. It really makes them come alive!

Villains

Of course, you need bad guys, too!

Here are some bad guys for you to try. Draw them taking on your hero.

Check out these robots!
They aren't human, but you
can draw them with the
sticks and circles that you
used for drawing humans.
Here are a few for you to
practice with.

Robots

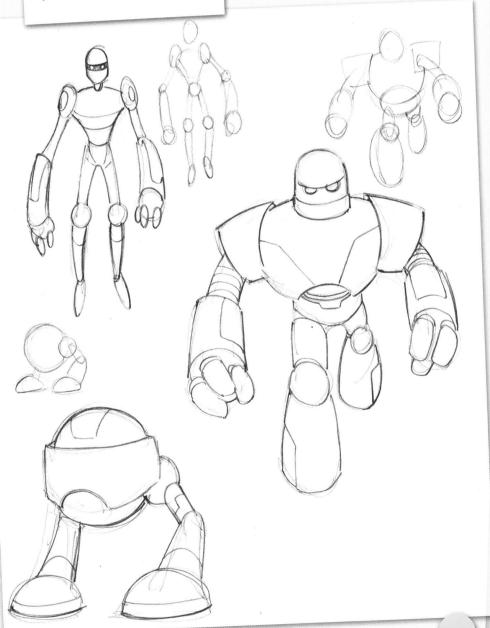

Backgrounds

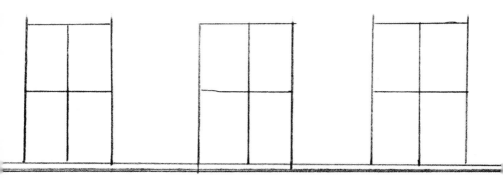

Backgrounds are the scenes that your characters are in. Backgrounds can be anything from a city scene to a country scene, or even another world scene! Here are some backgrounds for you to try out with your characters, but be sure to create some of your very own. Sketch in some characters right here on this page!

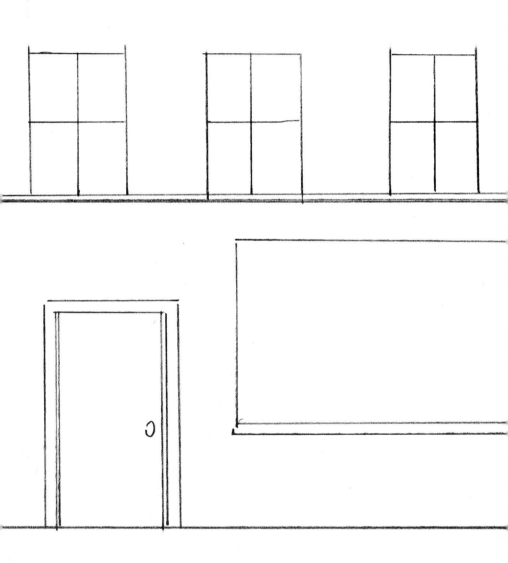

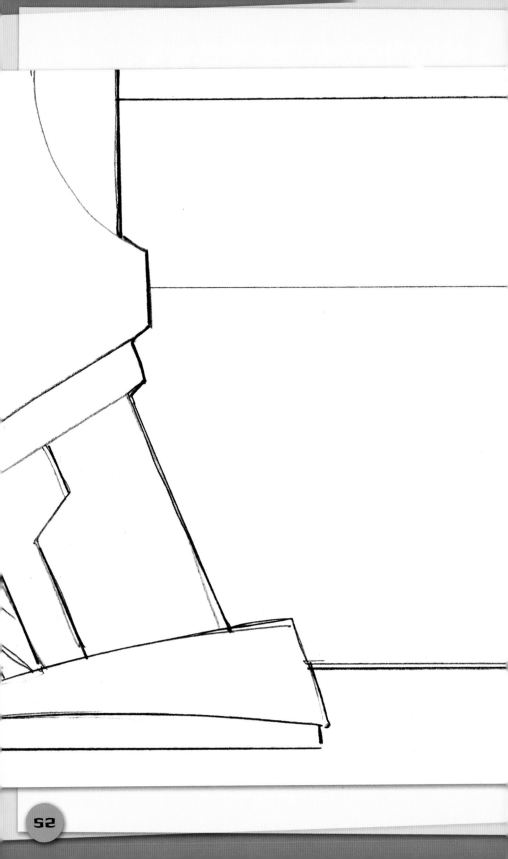

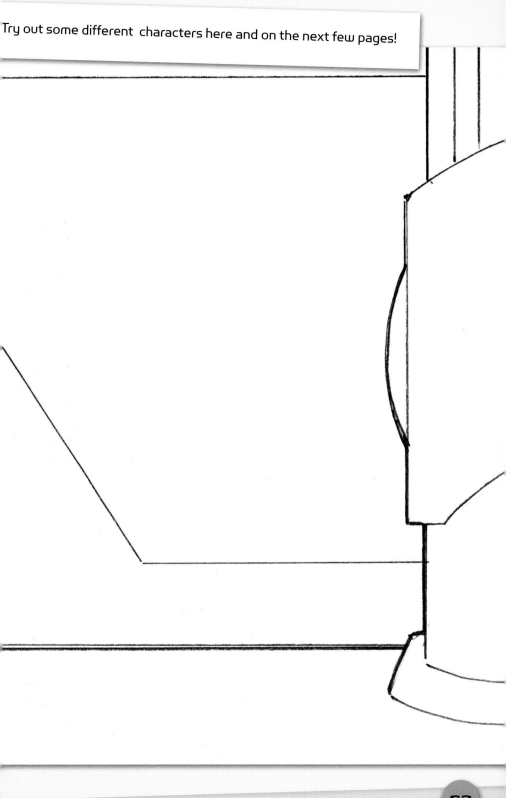

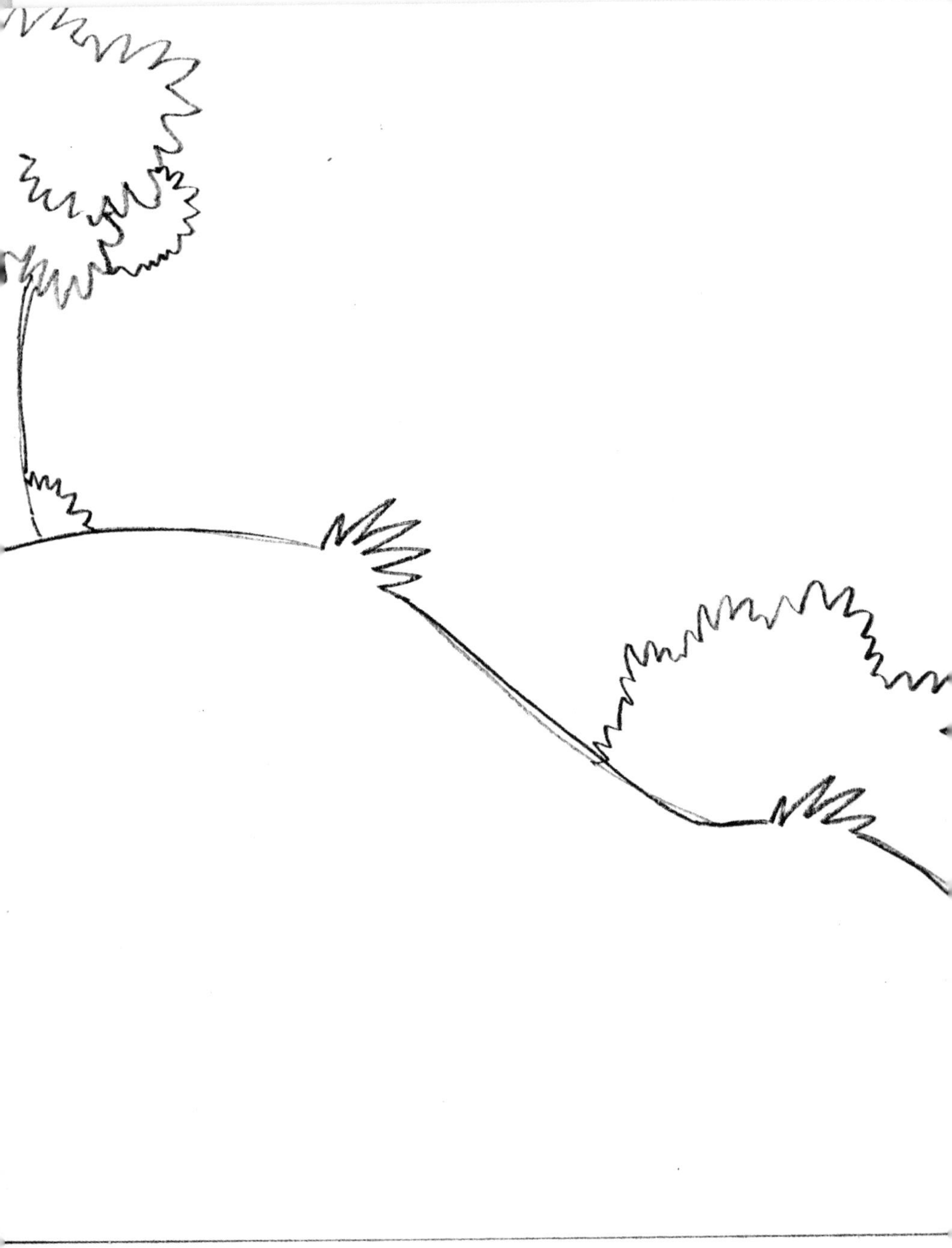

The Big Finale!

Now you can use everything you've learned and put it all together to draw the characters in action with each other. Check out these examples!

Captain Space and
Kid Hero

Hunter and Archer

Cat Girl and Gray Thunder

The End

You've done it! Great job!
It's a lot of fun making up your own characters,
so now strike out on your own!
Remember your character can be anyone
and do anything. There is no limit to your
imagination. Draw manga characters of your
friends and family! Keep practicing –
the more you draw, the better you get!

The most important thing to do is have fun!